Unlock the secrets of successful small business marketing on a shoestring budget with this comprehensive guide! Packed with over 60 actionable strategies, you'll learn cost-effective DIY methods for creating a recognizable brand, establishing a strong online presence, mastering content and SEO, implementing impactful local marketing tactics, and analyzing your efforts with goal tracking and metrics. Whether you're a solopreneur or a small team, this book is your go-to resource for building a thriving business without breaking the bank. Perfect for entrepreneurs seeking practical marketing solutions, branding insights, and digital presence strategies. Don't miss out on this essential guide to elevate your small business to new heights! #SmallBusinessMarketing #DIYMarketing #BudgetFriendlyBranding

DIY Business Marketing on a Shoestring Budget
60+ Actionable DIY Strategies
© 2024 Elena Pemberton
ISBN: 9798876970480

What others are saying:

Elena Pemberton will forever have a positive impact on my approach to business. Her perspectives were thoughtful and insightful, and her communication style was balanced with candor and professionalism. My coaching with Elena began when I faced a new opportunity to become a company owner vs. an employee. Transitioning into a new role thrust me into responsibilities that were previously unfamiliar to me. Her experience and viewpoints were extremely helpful to me in strengthening my focus and commitment to delivering a consistent product and experience. I was also challenged to balance risk-taking with accountability. My time with Elena has influenced my professional development, positively impacting my direct organization and our end consumers.
- Amanda Cox,
AUSTIN DECORATIVE CONCRETE SOLUTIONS

"Elena has encouraged me to start my own business and coached and supported me over the last year. Her innovation helps me to course-correct by making slight adjustments to continue the growth of my business. I appreciate how she challenges me to expand and helps me problem-solve through my objections. She's not only an advisor but a great mentor and creativity coach!
Forever grateful"
- Kathleen Witek,
GARDEN DISTRICT STL

"Incredibly professional and knowledgeable! By spending time with me discussing my current business needs, as well as my future plans, she provided me with up-to-date information and experience so I can properly build a foundation for success! I definitely recommend!"
- Rommel Good,
RORSHAX MUSIC

THE IDEAL PROFESSIONAL SPEAKER FOR YOUR NEXT EVENT!

◆

Challenging people to find business opportunities in their obstacles

Invite Elena Pemberton
for a keynote and/or workshop training!
To contact or book Elena Pemberton
to speak:

connect@elpemberton.com
www.elpemberton.com

Contents

Introduction ✦ DIY Business Marketing on a Shoestring Budget

The Importance of Marketing for Small Business Success

The self-marketing journey can be overwhelming and daunting for many small business owners and entrepreneurs. After pouring life savings into launching a business, the pressure to attract customers and maintain a steady revenue stream becomes incessant.

Here's the hard truth: No matter how brilliant your business idea, how incredible your product, or how valuable your service is, they risk fading into obscurity without effective marketing. Marketing serves as the vital puzzle piece that bridges the gap between the work you do and the revenue essential for survival. Without it, your potential customers wouldn't be aware of your existence.

However, a surprising number of small business owners resist investing in marketing. They might claim it's too expensive or perceive it as a diversion of funds that could be better spent on improving their products or services. They may not realize that marketing is the most scalable form of growth.

While perfecting your offerings is undoubtedly crucial, even the best product or service needs marketing to drive sales.

Goal 4
Additional Brand-Building Strategies

Define Your Brand Story

Craft a compelling origin narrative that goes beyond the surface. Share the story of your company, founding team, or initial vision across various platforms. This narrative engages customers and clarifies what your brand stands for.

Spotlight Your Team

Humanize your business by showcasing the people behind it. Share team members' stories, their expertise, and behind-the-scenes footage of your operations and customer service. This personal touch builds a connection and adds authenticity to your brand.

Free Content & Guides

Build authority within your industry by offering valuable free content. From email newsletters and ebooks to toolkits, these lead magnets establish your expertise and provide avenues to initiate conversations with ideal clients.

Cohesive Website Design

Your website is a digital storefront. Ensure its information architecture, layout, visuals, and copywriting align with the personality behind your brand. Consistency in look, feel, and messaging should be evident at first glance, creating a seamless online brand experience.

Demystifying DIY Marketing on a Budget

This guide aims to demystify DIY marketing for small business owners operating on a shoestring budget. Throughout this comprehensive guide, you will discover actionable strategies covering various aspects of marketing. From creating a recognizable brand identity to establishing a robust online presence, this guide aims to equip you with the knowledge and tools needed to market your business effectively without breaking the bank.

What You'll Learn

1. **Creating a Recognizable Brand Identity for Free**
   - Uncover the essentials of crafting a brand identity that stands out.
   - Utilize cost-effective methods to establish a brand that resonates with your audience.

2. **Easy Website Setup, Blogging Strategies, Social Media Tips**
   - Navigate the process of setting up a user-friendly website without a hefty budget.
   - Learn effective blogging strategies to engage your audience.

3. **The Power of Content and SEO to Attract Ideal Customers**
   - Harness the potential of content marketing and SEO to draw in your target audience.
   - Learn how to create valuable content that resonates with your customers.

4. **Local Marketing Tactics to Embed Yourself in the Community**
   - Explore cost-effective local marketing tactics to become an integral part of your community.
   - Leverage strategies to enhance your visibility and connection with local customers.

5. **Analyzing Your Efforts Through Goal Tracking and Metrics**
   - Understand the significance of tracking goals and metrics in your marketing efforts.
   - Learn how to analyze your marketing performance to make informed decisions.

Your Complete Small Business Marketing Education

This guide comprises over 50 actionable strategies spanning branding, digital presence, creative content production, local outreach, contests, partnerships, events, and analytics. We've meticulously curated a comprehensive resource to empower you with the knowledge and tools necessary for effective small-business marketing.

Let's embark on this journey together, arming you with the insights and strategies to elevate your business. Whether you're a solopreneur or a small team, these DIY marketing techniques will pave the way for success on a shoestring budget.

Let's begin...

Chapter 1: Build Your Brand - Crafting a Distinct Identity

Your brand is the heartbeat of your business, a living entity that extends far beyond a mere logo or tagline. It encompasses the essence of your enterprise, shaping its personality, vision, and the emotional connection it forges with people. In this comprehensive chapter, we embark on a journey to explore the fundamental elements of branding that any small business owner can embrace without the need for a substantial marketing budget.

Goal 1:	Logos/Color Scheme: The Face of Your Identity
Goal 2:	DIY Visual Brand Assets: Extending Beyond Logos
Goal 3:	Affordable Merchandise: Powering Brand Equity
Goal 4:	Additional Brand-Building Strategies

Goal 1
Logos/Color Scheme: The Face of Your Identity

Establishing Identity

The visual components of your brand play a pivotal role in establishing a solid identity. Kickstart this process by crafting a unique logo design, utilizing accessible tools like Canva or LogoMaker. Choose elements that resonate with your personality and mirror the essence of your business offerings.

Color Harmony

Colors evoke emotions and create a visual identity. Select a palette of 1-3 associated colors that mirror your style. These chosen colors become the thread weaving through your business collateral, from websites and signs to packaging, creating a cohesive and memorable visual experience for your audience.

Consistency Across Touchpoints

Consistency is critical to reinforcing your brand identity. Maintain uniformity in fonts, icons, and overall branding across various touchpoints. This cohesiveness ensures a unified and recognizable brand experience for your audience.

Goal 2
DIY Visual Brand Assets: Extending Beyond Logos

Beyond Logos

Extend your visual branding beyond logos to create a holistic brand experience. Utilize platforms like Canva, Venngage. or basic software like PowerPoint to craft visually appealing assets. These can include social media banners/profile pictures, website header images, email newsletter templates, and signage.

Creative Imagery

Visual content is a powerful storytelling tool. Get creative with photography by capturing stylized images that authentically represent your business. These images can be used across a spectrum of promotional materials, from advertisements to flyers, adding a personal touch to your brand communication.

Goal 3
Affordable Merchandise: Powering Brand Equity

Powerful Giveaways

Invest in promotional giveaways as tangible expressions of your brand. Custom t-shirts, mugs, stickers, or packaging seamlessly integrated with your branding act as influential ambassadors. Research local printing options or leverage vendors like Vistaprint and Stickermule for cost-effective custom orders.

Brand Equity at Low Cost

Affordable merchandise serves as a catalyst, enhancing brand equity at a low cost. These items leave a lasting impression on your audience, fostering a connection that goes beyond transactions.

Signage & Packaging

Even seemingly simple elements like customized packaging, bags, labels, and store signage play a crucial role in reinforcing brand retention. Use these collateral items strategically as reminders of your brand, creating a memorable and cohesive brand environment.

Reviews & Testimonials

Leverage the power of social proof through proactive efforts to collect reviews, testimonials, and referrals from satisfied customers. Their voices become powerful tools to introduce your offerings to new visitors, building trust and credibility.

In this comprehensive chapter, we have delved into the foundational elements of building a strong brand. From visual components to storytelling and engagement strategies, these elements collectively shape the identity of your business. Stay tuned for the next chapter, where we will dive into the practical steps to implement these strategies and bring your brand to life.

Practical Implementation Strategies:
Bringing Your Bake Shop Brand to Life

✦

Now that we've laid the delicious groundwork for your home-based bake shop brand, it's time to roll up our sleeves and put these branding strategies into action. Below are practical implementation strategies that will turn your brand vision into a mouthwatering reality.

1. Logo Unveiling Campaign: Sweet Teasers
Launch an enticing campaign on social media to unveil your newly crafted logo. Tease your audience with behind-the-scenes glimpses and sneak peeks of the design process. Create a sense of anticipation and excitement as you build up to the grand reveal.

Action Steps:
- Share teaser images or videos on Instagram and Facebook.
- Use countdowns in your stories to create a sense of anticipation.
- Engage with your audience by asking for their guesses about the logo.

2. Color Palette Showcase: Tasting the Rainbow
Introduce your selected color palette in a visually appealing way. Create vibrant and tempting social media posts showcasing your chosen colors. Incorporate these colors into your posts, stories, and any visual content you share to establish a consistent and appetizing look.

Action Steps:
- Dedicate a series of posts to each color in your palette.
- Share images of your baked goods that highlight these colors.
- Encourage followers to share their favorite color-inspired treats.

3. Consistency Across Platforms: Baking on Brand
Ensure consistency in branding across all your digital platforms. Update your website, social media profiles, and any online presence to reflect

the new visual identity. Use uniform fonts, icons, and styling to create a seamless and delightful online experience.

Action Steps:
- Update profile pictures and cover photos with the new logo.
- Adjust website colors and visuals to align with the color palette.
- Create a brand style guide for easy reference and consistency.

4. Visual Content Bonanza: Mouthwatering Moments
Launch a visual content campaign featuring your delectable treats. Use the visual assets created through Canva, Venngage, or PowerPoint to craft stunning images. Highlight these visuals in your social media posts, stories, and even on your website.

Action Steps:
- Create a series of visually appealing posts showcasing your baked goods.
- Experiment with different layouts and designs for variety.
- Encourage followers to share their favorite treats using a branded hashtag.

5. Branded Merchandise Rollout: Sweet Swag Surprise
Introduce your branded merchandise with a special rollout. Offer limited-edition items or discounts for the first customers who purchase merchandise. Make it an event, both online and, if applicable, at your physical location.

Action Steps:
- Showcase merchandise in visually appealing posts and stories.
- Run a countdown to the merchandise launch.
- Encourage customer engagement by asking them to share photos with the new merchandise.

6. Brand Storytelling Series: Baking Narratives
Initiate a brand storytelling series across your various platforms. Share captivating stories about the origins of your bake shop, the team members involved, and the unique journey behind your delicious creations. Connect with your audience on a personal level.

Action Steps:
- Craft engaging posts, articles, or even short videos about your brand story.
- Share anecdotes and behind-the-scenes moments.
- Encourage customer interaction by asking them to share their favorite stories or memories related to your bake shop.

7. Free Content Offerings: Recipe Riches

Initiate your authority-building strategy with free content offerings. Launch a series of recipe newsletters, baking guides, or toolkits. Share these valuable resources through your website and social media to position your bake shop as an expert in the world of baking.

Action Steps:
- Create visually appealing graphics promoting your free content.
- Implement a sign-up form on your website for newsletters.
- Encourage followers to share their baking experiences using your recipes.

8. Cohesive Website Transformation: Digital Confectionery Makeover

Revamp your website to reflect the cohesive brand experience you've envisioned. Ensure that the layout, visuals, and copy align with the personality of your brand. Implement the changes gradually, creating a seamless transition.

Action Steps:
- Update website visuals and colors according to the new brand guidelines.
- Ensure that the copywriting mirrors the tone and voice of your brand.
- Test website functionality to guarantee a smooth user experience.

9. Signage & Packaging Showcase: Branded Delight

Highlight your customized packaging, labels, and store signage as integral elements of your brand. Share images and stories on social media about how these elements enhance the overall brand experience for your customers.

Action Steps:
- Create visually appealing posts showcasing your packaging and

signage.

- Share customer testimonials or reactions to the branded elements.
- Run a campaign encouraging customers to share photos of their purchases with the branded packaging.

10. Reviews & Testimonials Activation: Sweet Voices
Initiate a proactive campaign to collect reviews and testimonials from your satisfied customers. Encourage them to share their experiences on Google, Facebook, or other review platforms. Leverage these positive voices to build trust and credibility.

Action Steps:
- Request reviews through personalized emails or in-store signage.
- Create engaging social media posts featuring snippets from positive reviews.
- Offer incentives or discounts for customers who share their feedback.

Congratulations on embarking on this flavorful journey to bring your bake shop brand to life! By implementing these practical strategies, you'll not only establish a strong brand presence but also create a delightful and memorable experience for your customers.

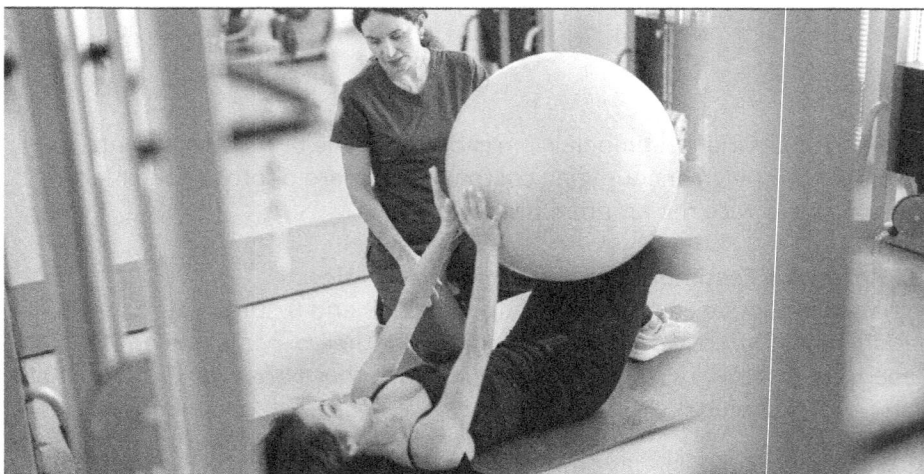

Chapter 2: Crafting Your Digital Presence - Detailed Guide

In the rapidly evolving business landscape, having a robust online presence is imperative for small businesses. This chapter provides a detailed guide on creating and optimizing your digital footprint, encompassing a website, blogging, email marketing, and social media strategies.

Goal 1:	Website and Blogging
Goal 2:	Email Marketing
Goal 3:	Social Media Marketing
Goal 4:	Optimizing Your Digital Presence

Goal 1
Website and Blogging

Affordable Foundation

Acquiring Domain and Hosting
Invest in a domain name and a simple hosting plan, costing less than $100 for the first year. This lays the foundation for your digital real estate.

WordPress Installation
Install WordPress, a user-friendly platform, for hassle-free customization of your website.

Core Pages Design
Design a visually appealing site with core pages like Home, About, Contact, and a Blog section.

Content is King

Regular Blogging
Commit to publishing regular, long-form blog content. This not only showcases your expertise but also contributes to improving your website's SEO.

Diverse Content
Share diverse content, including advice, behind-the-scenes insights, industry updates, or local events.

Calls-to-Action
Incorporate clear calls-to-action (CTAs) within your blog content to guide visitors toward desired actions, whether contacting your business or purchasing.

Goal 2
Email Marketing

Building Relationships

Email Capture
Every business needs an email list to foster repeat business. Start capturing emails strategically across your website and social channels.

MailChimp Utilization
Leverage MailChimp's free plan, accommodating up to 2,000 contacts. Utilize it to send out monthly newsletters and special offers, enticing customers to return.

Goal 3
Social Media Marketing

Active Presence

Platform Selection
Maintain an active presence on major platforms like Facebook and Instagram, engaging with audiences where they spend their time.

Content Diversity
Post diverse content, including impactful visuals and valuable commentary.

Cross-Promotion
Cross-promote your blog content on social media platforms to drive traffic back to your website.

Advertising Experimentation
Experiment with affordable daily ads, with budgets ranging from $5-10, to further amplify your organic content.

Platform-Specific Strategies

Instagram Focus
As Instagram is highly visual, focus on sharing photos and reels that showcase your products or services. Leverage hashtags and tags to extend your reach.

Facebook Precision
Utilize Facebook's precise targeting options for paid ads. Laser-focus on location, interests, and behaviors to maximize conversion potential.

Retargeting Strategies
Implement retargeting strategies across multiple channels to re-engage visitors who have interacted with your business.

Goal 4
Optimizing Your Digital Presence

Meaningful Conversations

Website Setup

WordPress Installation:
Install WordPress for ease of use and customization.

Core Pages Creation:
Develop essential pages like Home, About, Contact, and
Services/Products.

Blogging
Regular Blogging: Commit to publishing at least one blog post per week.

Local Presence
Google My Business Listing: Boost local discoverability by securing a
Google My Business listing.

Social Media Accounts
Platform Diversification: Create accounts on major platforms, including
Facebook, Instagram, LinkedIn, and Twitter.

Content Sharing
Consistent Engagement: Regularly share visual and written content
across your social media accounts.

Paid Advertising
Budgeted Ads: Run Facebook and Instagram ads with a daily budget of
$5 to maximize cost-effectiveness.

Email Marketing
Newsletter Implementation: Enable email signups on your website and utilize a free MailChimp account to send a monthly newsletter.

Calls-to-Action
Strategic CTAs: Integrate calls-to-action across all online properties to guide user actions.

By following these detailed steps, you'll establish a solid digital presence, fostering engagement and building credibility. This foundation sets the stage for advanced strategies that will be explored in subsequent chapters. Stay tuned for insights on further elevating your online presence and achieving sustainable growth for your small business.

Practical Implementation Strategies:
Establishing Your Digital Presence as a Wellness Coach

✦

Affordable Foundation

Now that we've explored the comprehensive chapter on creating and optimizing your digital presence, let's delve into practical implementation strategies. These steps will help you establish a robust online presence, reaching and engaging with your target audience effectively.

1. Acquiring Domain and Hosting:

- Choose a domain name that reflects your wellness coaching brand.
- Invest in a hosting plan, ensuring it aligns with your budget and business needs.

2 WordPress Installation:

- Install WordPress for a user-friendly platform that facilitates customization.

3. Core Pages Design:

- Craft visually appealing pages such as Home, About, Contact, and a dedicated Blog section on your WordPress site.
- Select a theme that resonates with the holistic and wellness-oriented nature of your coaching services.

4. Content is King

- o Develop a content calendar for regular blog posts focusing on wellness tips, personal insights, industry trends, and local wellness events.

5. Calls-to-Action (CTAs):

- o Strategically place CTAs within your blog content, encouraging readers to explore personalized wellness programs or schedule a coaching session.

6. Core Pages Design:

- o Craft visually appealing pages such as Home, About, Contact, and a dedicated Blog section on your WordPress site.
- o Select a theme that resonates with the holistic and wellness-oriented nature of your coaching services.

Practical Implementation Strategies:
Nurturing Client Relationships through Email Marketing

✦
Building Relationships

1. Platform Selection:

- Identify key social media platforms where your target audience actively seeks wellness content – focus on platforms like Instagram and Facebook.

2. Content Diversity:

- Share visually appealing images, informative videos, and insightful commentary aligned with wellness principles.
- Promote your blog content on social media to drive traffic and engagement.

3. Advertising Experimentation:

- Experiment with affordable daily ads on Facebook and Instagram, with budgets ranging from $5-10, to amplify your wellness coaching content.

4. Platform-Specific Strategies:

- Leverage Instagram's visual appeal for showcasing wellness practices, such as meditation or healthy recipes, using relevant wellness hashtags.
- Utilize Facebook's precise targeting for ads, focusing on users interested in holistic health and wellness.

5. Retargeting Strategies:

- o Implement retargeting pixels on your website to re-engage visitors interested in your wellness coaching services.

Practical Implementation Strategies:

Optimizing Your Digital Presence for Wellness Coaching Success

✦

Meaningful Conversations

1. Website Setup:

- Optimize your WordPress installation to reflect the serene and inviting nature of your wellness coaching services.
- Ensure core pages provide clear information about your holistic approach, coaching philosophy, and available programs.

2. Blogging:

- Commit to a consistent blogging schedule, sharing wellness tips, success stories, and transformative experiences at least once a week.

3. Local Presence:

- Enhance local discoverability by creating and optimizing your Google My Business listing with a focus on wellness offerings.

4. Social Media Accounts:

- Diversify your presence across major platforms such as Facebook, Instagram, LinkedIn, and Twitter, emphasizing wellness content.

5. Content Sharing:

- Regularly share engaging visual and written content across all social media accounts to foster a sense of community around wellness.

6. Paid Advertising:

- Continue experimenting with budgeted Facebook and Instagram ads, highlighting personalized wellness coaching programs and benefits.

7. Email Marketing:

- Ensure seamless integration of email signups on your website, offering exclusive wellness content to subscribers.
- Regularly send out newsletters with valuable insights, holistic wellness practices, and special coaching offers.

8. Calls-to-Action:

- Strategically place CTAs across your website and social media to guide users toward scheduling a wellness consultation or joining a coaching program.

By following these specialized steps, you'll establish a robust digital presence as a health and wellness coach, fostering engagement and credibility in the wellness community. This foundational strategy sets the stage for advanced wellness coaching strategies to be explored in subsequent chapters. Stay tuned for insights on further elevating your online presence and achieving sustainable growth for your wellness coaching practice.

Chapter 3: Content Marketing

✦

Welcome to Chapter 3, where we delve into the art and science of Content Marketing. This powerful strategy involves consistently creating and distributing valuable, relevant content to attract and retain a clearly defined target audience. Content marketing builds loyalty, fosters engagement, and acts as a magnet for new customers through search engines and social sharing.

Goal 1:   SEO and Keywords

Goal 2:   Blogging

Goal 3:   Video

Goal 4:   Podcasting

Goal 5:   Topics to Cover

Goal 6:   Formats People Love

Goal 7:   Implementation Strategies

Goal 1
SEO and Keywords

Understand Audience Queries

Begin by researching what your potential customers actively search for—answers, inspiration, and solutions. Identify a shortlist of precise keywords and questions to optimize your content for.

Organic Integration

Integrate these keywords organically within your content—in writing, page metadata, or alt text. This ensures that your content is found on search engines like Google and recommended when people ask related queries.

Goal 2
Blogging

Consistent Publishing

Publish blog posts at least 1-2 times per month. Cover various topics, including FAQs, how-to advice, local events, behind-the-scenes imagery, and profile features.

Varied Multimedia Content

Incorporate varied multimedia content types to retain visitor interest. Make your styling digestible through the use of bullet points, charts, infographics, and other visual elements rather than presenting heavy blocks of text.

GOAL 3

Goal 3
Video

Engaging Visual Storytelling

Create informal tutorial videos, product explainers, and founder introduction videos. Video content is a powerful tool for conveying helpful information quickly through engaging visual storytelling.

GOAL 4

Goal 4
Podcasting

Long-Form Value-Added Content

Explore longer-form content through podcasting. Start by interviewing past customers, partners, and community members to showcase the depth of expertise around common pain points.

Goal 5
Topics to Cover

Beyond the Obvious

Go beyond the obvious to intrigue visitors. Share actionable tips, compile stats and data, create templates/calculators as resources, and highlight local partners.

Goal 6
Formats People Love

Diverse Multimedia

Utilize a mix of content formats, including videos, stats, checklists, and interviews. Enable easy skimming with ample multimedia content.

Goal 7
Implementation Strategies

Help, Don't Just Sell

Remember, the more you help versus directly selling, the further your content can spread organically, building trust along the way.

1. Research Target Audience Questions and Pain Points
   o Dig deep into what your audience is searching for and what challenges they are facing.
2. Create Informational Blog Content Around These Topics
   o Craft informative blog posts addressing audience questions and pain points.
3. Use Free Tools Like the Hemingway App to Optimize your Writing
   o Enhance the readability of your content using tools like Hemingway App.
4. Format Posts with Headings, Lists, Images, Quotes
   o Improve the readability and visual appeal of your posts with effective formatting.
5. Get Legal Guest Blog Posts on Relevant Industry Sites
   o Collaborate with industry sites to publish guest blog posts and expand your reach.
6. Give Away Free Resource Guides and Checklists
   o Provide valuable resources to your audience in the form of guides and checklists.
7. Start Creating Educational YouTube Videos
   o Utilize YouTube as a platform for educational video content.
8. Customer Issues
   o Dive into long-form content through a business podcast, addressing customer issues.
9. Write and Optimize Titles, Meta Descriptions, Alt Text
   o Pay attention to the details—craft compelling titles, meta descriptions, and alt text.

10. Create Comparison Articles
    - Compare products or services to guide your audience in their decision-making.
11. Write "Best Of" Recommendations
    - Showcase your expertise by providing recommendations and best-of lists.
12. Share Company News Updates
    - Keep your audience informed and engaged with regular updates on company news.
13. Spotlight Uses for Products/Services
    - Showcase practical applications and use cases for your products or services.
14. Compare to Competitors
    - Offer objective comparisons to help customers make informed choices.
15. Encourage User-Generated Content
    - Foster engagement by encouraging your audience to contribute content.
16. Repurpose Content Across Formats
    - Maximize the value of your content by repurposing it across different formats.
17. Conduct Interesting Interviews
    - Engage your audience with insightful interviews that bring unique perspectives.

By implementing these strategies, you'll not only create compelling content but also establish a strong online presence that resonates with your target audience. Stay tuned for the next chapter, where we'll explore advanced techniques to elevate your content marketing game and drive sustainable growth for your small business.

Practical Implementation Strategies:
Brushing Colors into the Digital Canvas For Artists

✦

Welcome to the detailed content marketing strategy designed to amplify your presence as an artist. This comprehensive approach encompasses SEO, blogging, multimedia content, videos, podcasting, and actionable implementation steps to create an impactful online presence.

SEO and Keywords: Crafting a Findable Masterpiece

1. **Understand Audience Queries:**

   ○ Conduct in-depth research to unravel the queries, aspirations, and challenges of art enthusiasts actively searching for inspiration and solutions.

2. **Organic Integration:**

   ○ Seamlessly weave carefully chosen keywords into your content—captivating descriptions, image alt text, and metadata—ensuring discoverability on search engines.

Blogging: Strokes of Insightful Content

3. **Consistent Publishing:**

   ○ Establish a consistent schedule for sharing your artistic journey through blog posts and publishing insightful content at least 1-2 times monthly. Cover diverse topics, from frequently asked questions to behind-the-scenes revelations.

4. **Varied Multimedia Content:**

- Elevate visitor engagement by incorporating diverse multimedia content. Break down the visual barriers with digestible styling, using bullet points, charts, infographics, and other visual elements to complement your narrative.

Video: Breathing Life into Your Art

5. **Engaging Visual Storytelling:**

- Create captivating tutorial videos, share product explainers, and introduce yourself through engaging founder videos. Video content is a powerful medium for conveying artistic nuances and building a deeper connection with your audience.

Podcasting: Conversations on Canvas

6. **Long-Form Value-Added Content:**

- Explore the world of podcasting to provide long-form, value-added content. Showcase your expertise by interviewing past customers, collaborators, and community members, adding depth to your artistic insights.

7. **Topics to Cover: Beyond the Canvas:**

- Venture beyond the obvious. Share actionable tips, compile meaningful statistics and data, create templates and calculators as valuable resources, and highlight collaborations with local artistic partners.

Implementation Strategies: Painting the Roadmap

8. **Help, Don't Just Sell:**

- Prioritize being a helpful resource over direct selling. Your content should inspire, educate, and resonate with your audience.

9. **Research Target Audience Questions and Pain Points:**

   o Dive deep into the questions and challenges your audience faces in the world of art. Understand their pain points and aspirations.

10. **Create Informational Blog Content:**

    o Craft informative and visually appealing blog posts addressing audience questions and pain points. Make art accessible through your words.

11. **Use Free Tools for Optimization:**

    o Enhance the readability of your content using tools like Hemingway App. Ensure that your artistic expressions are conveyed effortlessly.

12. **Format Posts Effectively:**

    o Improve readability and visual appeal with effective formatting. Use headings, lists, images, and quotes to make your content visually engaging.

13. **Collaborate for Guest Blog Posts:**

    o Extend your reach by collaborating with relevant industry sites. Share your artistic journey through guest blog posts on platforms where your audience gathers.

14. **Provide Free Resource Guides:**

    o Offer valuable resources to your audience in the form of guides and checklists. Showcase your expertise and provide tools that resonate with aspiring artists.

15. **Start Creating Educational Videos:**

    o Utilize YouTube as a platform for educational video content. Share techniques, insights, and the stories behind your art.

16. Launch a Business Podcast:

- Dive into long-form content through a business podcast, addressing customer issues and discussing the broader world of art.

17. Optimize Titles and Descriptions:

- Pay meticulous attention to the details. Craft compelling titles, meta descriptions, and alt text. Optimize them to draw viewers into your artistic world.

By meticulously implementing these strategies, you'll create compelling content and establish a strong online presence that resonates with your target audience. Stay tuned for advanced techniques to elevate your content marketing game and drive sustainable growth for your small art business.

Chapter 4: Local Marketing Magic

In the digital age, having an online presence is crucial, but nothing beats the impact of local outreach. This chapter explores the strategies that make your business tangible to neighborhood customers, enticing them to visit your storefront or venue in person.

Goal 1:	Taking it to the Streets
Goal 2:	Signs & Visual Promos: Window to the Community
Goal 3:	Sponsor Community Events: Community Connection
Goal 4:	Reviews & Referrals: Word-of-Mouth Goldmine
Goal 5:	Advanced Local Marketing Strategies

Goal 1
Taking it to the Streets

Design and Print

Design attention-grabbing flyers using free templates on platforms like Canva. Print small batches inexpensively at local vendors or your nearest FedEx store.

Creative Distribution

Distribute creatively by having your team walk around popular public hotspots such as parks or markets, handing out flyers. Explore posting on community boards or using clipboard-hung flyers at local businesses (with permission).

Goal 2
Signs & Visual Promos: Window to the Community

Eye-Catching Displays

Utilize simple yet eye-catching signs, even if created using foam boards and markers, in your storefront windows or along busy streets. Regularly update these signs to advertise current deals and maintain a consistent branding look for instant recall.

Goal 3
Sponsor Community Events: Community Connection

Budget-Friendly Sponsorship

Engage with your community without breaking the bank. Offer to display logo banners at street fairs, co-sponsor contests at high school games, or donate raffle items for charity galas. The goodwill generated goes a long way in building community connections.

Goal 4
Reviews & Referrals: Word-of-Mouth Goldmine

Proactive Engagement

Reach out proactively to happy customers for online reviews on platforms like Google and Facebook. Encourage word-of-mouth referrals to friends, leveraging the invaluable social proof for potential local customers.

Incentivize Activity

Motivate your customers by offering incentives like discounts for referrals and reviews. Even a few quality reviews can establish legitimacy and trust among potential patrons.

Goal 5
Advanced Local Marketing Strategies

Claim Local Business Listings

Ensure your business is listed on local directories like Yelp, enhancing your online visibility.

Run Local Social Media Ads

Target your local audience with ads on platforms like Facebook, utilizing city and interest-based targeting.

Sponsorship Beyond Events

Extend your sponsorship to activities like little league teams or community charity events, reinforcing your presence.

Educational Seminars and Workshops

Hold free seminars or workshops to showcase your expertise and engage with the local community.

Networking and Partnerships

Participate in local business expos, events, and partner with complementary local businesses for mutual benefit.

Direct Mail Postcards

Send direct mail postcards to local residents, offering targeted promotions and information.

Free Samples and Giveaways

Distribute free samples and organize giveaways to create excitement and attract local attention.

Run Local Social Media Ads

Target your local audience with ads on platforms like Facebook, utilizing city and interest-based targeting.

Networking Mixers

Host networking mixers to connect with the local business community and potential customers.

Run Direct Response Ads

Implement direct response ads to prompt immediate action from your local audience.

Graffiti Marketing

Explore unconventional methods like graffiti marketing to leave a lasting impression on the local scene.

Location Check-ins

Encourage customers to check in at your location on social media, boosting your visibility.

The more creative and consistent your local touchpoints, the more you stay front-of-mind for neighborhood patrons as service needs arise. Location-based marketing brings valuable foot traffic and establishes a lasting bond with your community. In the next chapter, we'll explore advanced techniques to elevate your local marketing game and drive sustained growth for your small business.

Practical Implementation Strategies:
Local Marketing As An Author

✦

Welcome to a comprehensive local marketing strategy tailored to authors seeking to captivate their neighborhood audience. In this chapter, we'll explore innovative approaches, from flyers to advanced strategies, to make your literary presence tangible within your local community.

Flyers: Taking it to the Streets

Design and Print:

Action Steps:
- Leverage Canva's user-friendly templates to design vibrant flyers showcasing your latest book covers, author events, or promotions.
- Print small batches locally to minimize costs, utilizing services like FedEx or nearby print shops.

Creative Distribution:

Action Steps:
- Deploy your team or enthusiastic volunteers to distribute flyers strategically.
- Target popular public spaces such as parks, local markets, and community events.
- Seek permission to display flyers on community boards or collaborate with local businesses for distribution.

Signs & Visual Promos: Window to the Community

Eye-Catching Displays:

Action Steps:
- Design visually appealing signs featuring captivating book covers, quotes, or endorsements.
- Place these signs in your storefront windows or along busy streets to capture the attention of passersby.
- Regularly update signs to showcase new releases, promotions, or upcoming events.

Sponsor Community Events: Community Connection

Budget-Friendly Sponsorship:

Action Steps:
- Identify local events, high school games, or charity galas that align with your target audience.
- Offer budget-friendly sponsorship by displaying banners, donating books, or co-sponsoring contests.

Advanced Local Marketing Strategies

Claim Local Business Listings:

Action Steps:
- Ensure your author profile is accurately listed on local directories like Yelp, Yellow Pages, and local business associations.

Run Local Social Media Ads:

Action Steps:
- Develop targeted Facebook ads to promote book launches, signings, or exclusive local events.
- Utilize city and interest-based targeting to ensure your ads reach the intended local audience.

Sponsorship Beyond Events:

Action Steps:
- Extend your sponsorship to local book clubs, libraries, or literary organizations.
- Host book-related activities or discussions to strengthen your ties with the local literary community.

Educational Seminars and Workshops:

Action Steps:
- Collaborate with local libraries, schools, or community centers to organize free literary workshops or seminars.
- Focus on topics that align with your expertise as an author and cater to the interests of the local audience.

Networking and Partnerships:

Action Steps:
- Attend local literary events, book expos, or book fairs to connect with fellow authors, readers, and potential collaborators.
- Forge partnerships with local bookstores or businesses that align with your genre or writing style.

Direct Mail Postcards:

Action Steps:
- Extend your sponsorship to local book clubs, libraries, or literary organizations.
- Host book-related activities or discussions to strengthen your ties with the local literary community.

Free Samples and Giveaways:

Action Steps:
- Distribute free book samples or organize giveaways at local fairs, farmers' markets, or community gatherings.
- Encourage attendees to engage with your work and spread the word about your books.

Networking Mixers:

Action Steps:
- Attend local literary events, book expos, or book fairs to connect with fellow authors, readers, and potential collaborators.
- Forge partnerships with local bookstores or businesses that align with your genre or writing style.

Run Direct Response Ads:

Action Steps:
- Launch direct response ads on platforms like Facebook or Instagram, prompting immediate actions such as attending a book signing or purchasing a new release.

Graffiti Marketing:

Action Steps:
- Collaborate with local street artists to create book-themed graffiti in strategic locations.
- Use this unconventional method to leave a lasting and visually striking impression on the local scene.

Location Check-ins:

Action Steps:
- Encourage readers to check in at your author events or book signings on social media platforms.
- Leverage location-based marketing to boost online visibility and create a sense of community.

By meticulously implementing these detailed steps, you'll enhance your local presence and cultivate a strong and supportive literary community around your work. This personalized and community-focused approach will contribute to sustained growth and increased visibility as an author within your local area.

Chapter 5: Analyzing Your Efforts

In the dynamic world of small business, many owners shy away from analytics or focus solely on activities they believe work, often missing opportunities for ongoing optimization. However, making informed, data-driven decisions is crucial for efficient growth, especially when operating on a shoestring budget.

Goal 1:	Google Analytics: Your Gateway to Insights
Goal 2:	Key Metrics to Track
Goal 3:	Always Be Testing
Goal 4:	Implementation Strategies

Goal 1
Google Analytics: Your Gateway to Insights
Centralized Dashboard

Google Analytics, a free platform, allows you to connect your website, social media, and other channels, providing a centralized dashboard with incredible visitor data—from traffic insights to purchase behavior.

Beginner's Guide

For beginners, the Acquisition tab is your starting point. Understand your highest traffic sources in the last 30 days, driving awareness. Experiment with channel comparisons to identify your most effective marketing channels.

Behavior Analysis

Delve into the Behavior tab, which showcases conversions. Set up goals such as contact form submissions, calls taken, or subscription signups. Understand the actions visitors take on your site.

Custom Dashboards

Leverage custom dashboards tailored to display metrics you care about the most. This provides a quick top-level view of what content and activities convert best. Regularly review and test changes in underperforming areas.

Goal 2
Key Metrics to Track

Choosing Wisely

From visitor traffic to email open rates, clicks on calls-to-action, and online/offline conversions—the metrics that showcase opportunities are endless. However, resist information overload. Define 2-3 key performance indicators (KPIs) directly aligned with revenue growth for simplicity.

Goal 3
Always Be Testing

Continuous Improvement

The beauty of thorough analytics lies in the constant discoveries and improvements you can make. if you identify blog post topics with high traffic but low engagement, adjust titles or featured images. Emails sent on Tuesdays outperforming Thursdays? Tweak your nurture sequence timing. Are Facebook followers ignoring "Call Now" posts? Try showcasing testimonials first.

Refine and Analyze

Refinement is a continuous process. Use marketing intelligence to save money while driving more sales.

Goal 4
Implementation Strategies

Install Free Google Analytics on Your Website

Begin by integrating Google Analytics on your website. This step is crucial to accessing comprehensive insights into your online performance.

Track and Assess Site Traffic and Engagement

Regularly monitor and assess site traffic and user engagement. Understand how visitors interact with your content and identify areas for improvement.

Review Top Landing/Exit Pages and Fix Issues

Identify your top landing and exit pages. Address any issues affecting the performance of these pages to enhance the overall user experience.

See Referrals and Best Marketing Channels

Explore the Referrals section in Google Analytics to identify your best marketing channels. Understand where your traffic is coming from and focus your efforts accordingly.

Set Up Dashboards for Key Metrics

Customize dashboards to display key metrics aligned with your business goals. This allows for a quick overview of your performance.

Measure Leads and Sales from Marketing Activities

Implement tracking mechanisms to measure leads and sales generated from your marketing activities. Understand the effectiveness of your campaigns.

Run Experiments Changing One Variable at a Time

Conduct experiments by changing one variable at a time. Test different campaign elements to identify what resonates best with your audience.

Evaluate Cost per Lead and Sale by Channel

Determine the cost per lead and sale for each marketing channel. Allocate resources efficiently based on the channels that provide the best return on investment.

Determine ROI for Paid Advertising Campaigns

Evaluate the return on investment (ROI) for your paid advertising campaigns. Understand the impact of your advertising spend on your bottom line.

Always Be Testing (Continued)

A/B test webpages, assess email open rates, experiment with altered ad copy, test send times and days, gauge social media engagement, review reader comments, survey customers directly, evaluate Net Promoter Score (NPS), assess chat completion rate, and track phone call leads through tracking and recording.

Mastering analytics empowers your small business to make informed decisions, optimize marketing efforts, and achieve efficient growth. Stay tuned for the conclusion, where we explore advanced strategies to further elevate your business to new heights.

Practical Implementation Strategies:
Analyzing Marketing Efforts

✦

An organic farmer can effectively apply and implement the strategies outlined in the marketing analytics chapter to gain insights, optimize efforts, and achieve efficient growth. Here's a step-by-step guide tailored for an organic farmer:

1. Install Free Google Analytics on Your Website

Action Steps:
- Ensure that your farm's website includes Google Analytics to track online performance.
- Track metrics such as website visitors, page views, and user engagement.

2. Track and Assess Site Traffic and Engagement

Action Steps:
- Monitor website traffic to specific pages, such as product listings, blog posts, or contact pages.
- Assess user engagement by analyzing the time spent on pages and interactions with content.

3. Review Top Landing/Exit Pages and Fix Issues

Action Steps:
- *Identify the most visited and exited pages, focusing on product pages or areas with high visitor drop-offs.*
- *Address issues like slow-loading product pages or unclear calls-to-action on landing pages.*

4. See Referrals and Best Marketing Channels

Action Steps:
- Identify referral sources to understand which online platforms or channels drive the most traffic.
- Focus on marketing efforts that align with the best-performing channels, such as social media or agricultural forums.

5. Set Up Dashboards for Key Metrics

Action Steps:
- Customize a Google Analytics dashboard to display key metrics like product page views, newsletter sign-ups, and overall site traffic.
- Regularly review this dashboard for a quick overview of performance.

6. Measure Leads and Sales from Marketing Activities

Action Steps:
- *Implement tracking mechanisms to measure leads and sales generated through online channels.*
- *Understand which marketing activities contribute to customer inquiries or product purchases.*

7. Run Experiments Changing One Variable at a Time

Action Steps:
- *Experiment with different product descriptions, visuals, or promotional offers on your website.*
- *Analyze how changes impact user behavior and adjust accordingly.*

8. Evaluate Cost per Lead and Sale by Channel

Action Steps:
- *Determine the cost per lead and sale for each marketing channel, including advertising costs on platforms like social media or local agriculture websites.*
- *Allocate resources based on the most cost-effective channels.*

9. Determine ROI for Paid Advertising Campaigns

Action Steps:
- Evaluate the return on investment (ROI) for any paid advertising campaigns.
- Understand the impact of advertising spend on the overall revenue generated from product sales.

10. Always Be Testing (Continued)

Action Steps:
- Continuously test different elements on your website and marketing materials.
- Gather feedback from customers and adjust your strategies based on insights gained.

By implementing these strategies, an organic farmer can make informed decisions, optimize marketing efforts, and achieve efficient growth, all while staying true to the principles of organic farming. Regular analysis and adaptation based on data-driven insights will contribute to the sustainability and success of the organic farming business.

In Conclusion ✦ Bringing It All Together

Bringing all the strategies together

After delving into numerous practical DIY marketing tactics across building your brand, crafting your online presence, content production, local outreach, and analyzing data, you may be feeling both inspired and overwhelmed. The key is to avoid the temptation to try doing everything at once, as this can lead to burnout and a lack of consistency. Remember, slow and steady progress wins the race.

Revisiting Core Business Goals

Start by revisiting your core business goals. Are you focused on brand awareness, lead generation, or local foot traffic? Choose 1-2 areas to focus on initially. Refer to the initial tactics outlined in those chapters as your starting roadmap.

The Power of Momentum

As you implement those first affordable activities across branding and content creation, maintain consistency. Set reminders to publish on social media twice weekly or send quarterly email newsletters. Consistency and gradually expanding efforts are key to building momentum.

Revisit What Works

Use the analytics tips to diligently measure what content formats, campaigns, and partnerships drive clicks, conversions, and sales. Rinse and repeat what proves effective while phasing out underperformers. No effort goes to waste as each data point is a valuable learning experience.

Next Level Growth

Over time, you will have built significant brand recognition, organic reach through followers sharing content, and loyalty through prior customer discounts. This foundation then allows you to expand into additional tactics like paid social advertising, guest podcast interviews on other brands, and hosting local co-marketing events. However, delay this next-level push initially while establishing your core offerings and voice through basic DIY activities first.

Stick with It!

Remember, the journey of a thousand miles begins with a single step. Consistent effort, strategic focus, and a willingness to adapt will lead to sustained growth and success for your small business. Embrace the journey, stay committed, and watch as your efforts yield remarkable results. Your business deserves it. Best of luck on your marketing adventure!

Marketing Plan

Method	Description	Budget
Write the marketing method here	Add a description of this method here	$123.00

Notes

Checklists

Weekly Items To Complete	Deadline	Completed?
Write an item to be completed here	8 June 2023	Yes

Monthly Items To Complete	Deadline	Completed?
Write an item to be completed here	8 June 2023	Yes

About The Author

Meet Elena Star, the founder of Monarch Marketing. Elena's entrepreneurial journey began with years of starting, selling, and supporting small businesses across different industries. Through her experiences, she came to a profound realization – the true heartbeat of any successful venture lies in its marketing strategy.

In the early days, Elena dabbled in various business ventures, learning the ins and outs of building something from the ground up. She witnessed the highs and lows of entrepreneurship and understood the pivotal role marketing played in the success of these endeavors.

One day, after successfully selling a business she had nurtured, Elena reflected on her entrepreneurial path. It became clear that her passion wasn't just about creating businesses but empowering others to thrive through effective marketing. She recognized that marketing was the linchpin that could elevate a business, irrespective of its nature.

This profound insight led Elena to channel her energy into starting Monarch Marketing. Her mission was no longer just about starting businesses; it was about helping others build and grow by mastering the art of marketing. Elena's approach is deeply rooted in the belief that businesses that make the world a better place deserve the chance to shine brightly through strategic and impactful marketing.

Now, at Monarch, Elena is dedicated to sharing her wealth of knowledge and experience with small business owners. She focuses on providing personalized consultations, educational workshops, and a resource hub filled with practical tools and templates. Elena's passion lies in empowering others to take control of their marketing efforts, turning their business dreams into tangible, sustainable success stories.

In Elena's world, the journey of entrepreneurship is intrinsically linked to the mastery of marketing, and she's committed to guiding others on this transformative path. Through Monarch Marketing, Elena Star is illuminating the way for small business owners, helping them confidently navigate the complexities of marketing and achieve the growth they've always envisioned.

More Resources

Introducing **"Bootstrap Your Business"** by Elena Star Pemberton, a comprehensive entrepreneurs journal that transforms how you approach your business. In this guide, Elena, an experienced entrepreneur, author, and business coach, shares invaluable insights gained from over 20 years of helping hundreds of individuals set up successful businesses.

Uncover the fundamental principles beyond having a great product or service. Elena emphasizes the importance of understanding your customers, identifying their problems, and offering resonating solutions. Through three thought processes, she guides you on transitioning from merely working for your business to creating a business you run.

1. **Customer-Centric Approach:** Shift your focus from the passion for your product to understanding what's important to your customer. Ask the crucial question, "What's in it for me?" to create a product that genuinely meets your customer's needs.

2. **Strategic Marketing:** Dispel the myth of "Build it and they will come." Elena underscores the necessity of promoting your product effectively. Learn how to showcase your solution and make potential customers aware of the incredible value you bring.

3. **Embracing Failure:** Recognize that failure is an option and understand that "done beats perfect." Elena provides practical advice on navigating the inevitable challenges of entrepreneurship, emphasizing the importance of learning from both successes and failures.

The journal offers a practical blueprint that allows you to apply these processes at any stage of your startup, minimizing trial and error. Elena's method, developed over years of successes and failures, provides a risk-free way to test and refine your business ideas.

By following this guide, you will:

Avoid Detours and Pitfalls: Sidestep common mistakes that can jeopardize your entrepreneurial dreams.

Successfully Launch Your Business: Validate and launch your business without the need to invest thousands of dollars in trial and error.

Apply Proven Methods: Benefit from tried-and-tested methods derived from the industry's most successful leaders.

Elena, who has successfully bootstrapped her own businesses with minimal resources, shares her expertise in scaling down to a minimum viable product, identifying your target market, crafting compelling messages, designing outstanding customer experiences, and creating a cycle of success.

"Bootstrap Your Business" is your go-to guide for turning your business dreams into reality, providing you with a roadmap for startup success even with the most limited resources. Say goodbye to unnecessary hurdles and hello to a thriving entrepreneurial journey.

Get your Entrepreneurs' Bullet Journal, "Bootstrap Your Business"

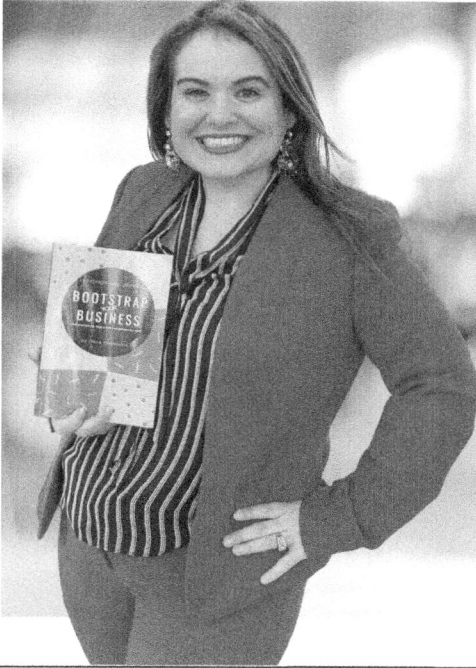

AVAILABLE AT AMAZON

✦

MonarchMarketingHub.com

CONNECT@ELPEMBERTON.COM

✦